History Snapshots

Children and World War II

Sarah Ridley

W

FRANKLIN WATTS

LONDON · SYDNEY

First published in 2007
by Franklin Watts

Copyright © Franklin Watts 2007

Franklin Watts
338 Euston Road
London NWI 3BH

Franklin Watts Australia
Level 17/207 Kent Street
Sydney, NSW 2000

Series editor: Sarah Peutrill
Art director: Jonathan Hair
Design: Jane Hawkins
Picture research: Fiona Orbell

A CIP catalogue record for this book is available from
the British Library.

Dewey no: 941.084
ISBN: 978 0 7496 7067 2

Printed in China

Franklin Watts is a division of Hachette Children's Books.

Picture credits:
Hulton Archive/Corbis: 27. Hulton Archive/Getty Images:
6, 7, 16. Imperial War Museum, London: 2, 11, 12, 13,
14t, 14b, 15c, 17, 18, 19t, 20, 21t, 22, 23t, 23c, 24, 25,
28. David Kindred: 15t, 26. Liverpool Central Library: 3,
10. National Army Museum, London: 8t, 8b. Popperfoto:
19c. 21c. Topfoto: 9.

Lyrics to 'White Cliffs of Dover' by Nat Burton

Every attempt has been made to clear copyright.
Should there be any inadvertent omission please apply
to the publisher for rectification.

White Cliffs of Dover

There'll be bluebirds over the white cliffs of Dover
Tomorrow, just you wait and see.
There'll be love and laughter and peace ever after
Tomorrow when the world is free.

Popular World War II song by Nat Burton

Contents

The war begins

In September 1939, the German army invaded Poland. Britain and France wanted to stop Germany from invading any more countries, so they declared war on Germany. Soon other countries joined the war, either on the German side or alongside France and Britain.

Date: 1939

The German army march into Poland. Before they invaded Poland, the Germans had already taken over Austria and Czechoslovakia (now the Czech Republic and Slovakia).

Adolf Hitler, the leader of the German people, wanted to make Germany really powerful by taking over other countries.

Date: 1937

Timeline

1934 Adolf Hitler becomes the leader of Germany.

1937 China and Japan are at war.

1939 World War II begins. Germany is on one side; Britain, France, Australia, New Zealand and Canada are on the other.

1940 Germany invades many countries in Europe. Italy and Japan join the war on the German side.

1941 The war spreads around the world. The USA joins the war on the British side. Germany attacks Russia.

1942 Battles rage around the world. Millions die.

1943–4 The British side begins to win more battles.

1945 War ends. The German side is defeated.

The army

When the war started, Britain sent its army to help defend France from the Germans. Many British men decided to join the armed forces. Others got letters from the government, telling them that they must join the forces.

Soldiers line up for inspection at an army training centre.

Date: 1941

A soldier learns how to cross a river on a rope. All across the country, men learnt how to fight, fly aeroplanes, drive tanks and sail huge ships.

Date: 1941

Date: 1939

A soldier father says goodbye to his baby. Many children hardly saw their fathers during the war.

Be a history detective

- Look for the long buildings in the training centre photo. These are where the men slept during their training.

- Ask your grandparents or great-grandparents whether they knew anyone who was a soldier in World War II.

Evacuation

The government feared that many children would be killed when German planes dropped bombs on cities. They decided to evacuate children to safer areas. Most of these children, called evacuees, went to live with strangers in the country.

Date: 1939

Evacuees rush to board a train. School children travelled with their teachers. They were only allowed to take a small suitcase, or rucksack, of clothes with them.

Evacuees on a nature walk. Some evacuees loved their new life, while thousands of others were miserable and soon returned home.

Date: 1941

Be a history detective

- Find the cardboard box that each child carried. This contained a gas mask (see page 15).
- How would it have felt to be evacuated?
- Find out whether children were evacuated from your area, or whether evacuees arrived from cities and towns.

School life

Children still had to go to school during the war. Teachers tried to keep life as normal as possible, but it could be difficult. There were not enough teachers, books, pens or paper.

Date: 1941

London school children continue lessons in a cellar classroom during an air raid (see page 14). Some city schools never evacuated their pupils, or had to reopen when many evacuees returned to live with their parents.

Evacuees of different ages learn their lessons in a village hall. In some areas, there were so few school places that children were taught in outdoor classrooms and village halls.

Date: 1940

Be a history detective

- Would you like your classroom to be in a cellar? What do you think it would be like?
- What are the children learning in the village hall schoolroom?

Preparing for air raids

The government warned the British people to expect attacks, called air raids, from German planes. Air-raid shelters were built to help protect people from bombs.

Date: 1943

People hung 'blackout' curtains at their windows to stop light from escaping at night. The government ordered a blackout so that everywhere would be dark and German bombers would not see the cities.

Children climb down into their air-raid shelter. People dug a big hole in the back garden and set up metal air-raid shelters.

Date: 1940

Schoolboys help to fill sandbags. These were piled up in front of buildings to help protect against bomb blasts.

Date: 1939

Date: 1941

Schoolchildren and their teacher practise wearing gas masks. The government gave everyone a gas mask in case the Germans dropped poisonous gas bombs.

Be a history detective

- Find the blackout curtains behind the ordinary curtains.
- Look at the school in the gas mask photo. How can you tell that bombs have dropped nearby?
- What do you think it felt like to wear a rubber gas mask?

The Blitz

Between September 1940 and May 1941, German planes bombed British cities almost every night. This was known as the Blitz. When a warning siren went off, people hurried to air-raid shelters.

Date: 1941

Children and their grandmother sit among the wreckage of their home in Liverpool. Many families lost everything in air raids and thousands of people died or were injured.

London firefighters try to put out a fire caused by German incendiary (fire) bombs. Some areas were completely destroyed by the Blitz.

Date: 1940

Be a history detective

- What has one child managed to hold onto during the air raid?

- Visit your local museum, or search the Internet to find out whether any bombs were dropped in your area during World War II.

Working women

As the men left for war, women took on their jobs. Some women trained as nurses, or learned to be firefighters or air-raid wardens. Women worked in factories, and on farms to help farmers grow food for everyone.

Female farm workers, known as 'Land Girls', help a farmer to load his truck with oats. Land Girls were part of the 'Land Army'.

Date: 1942

Date: 1941

Women factory workers make guns. Working mothers left their children in nurseries or asked other mothers to care for them.

An air-raid warden comforts a terrified child, after an air raid. Wardens checked the blackout, sounded air-raid sirens and helped out during and after air raids.

Date: c. 1943

Be a history detective

- Look at the clothes and hairstyles of the women in the photographs. They give clues about when the photo was taken.

- The people in the farming photo are using pitchforks to load the truck. What do farmers use today?

Food rationing

During the war, German submarines sank hundreds of ships carrying food to Britain. This caused food shortages. So, to share out what was available, everyone had a ration book. They contained coupons that allowed people to buy a set amount of rationed foods each week.

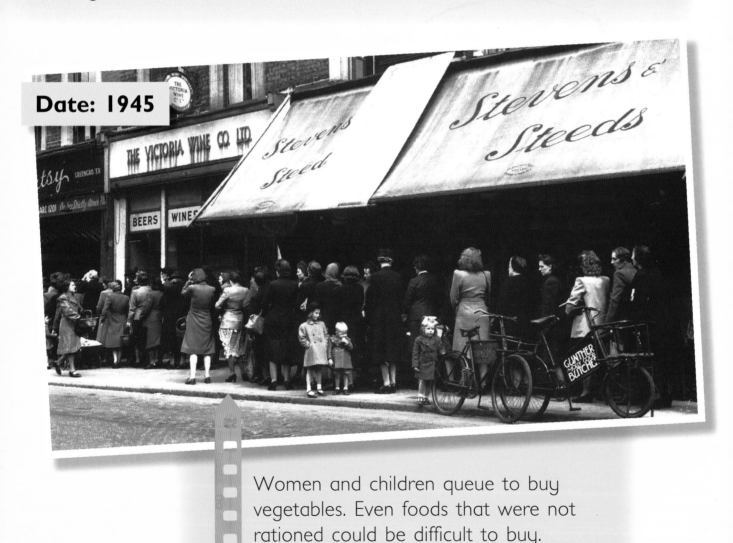

Date: 1945

Women and children queue to buy vegetables. Even foods that were not rationed could be difficult to buy.

The weekly rations for one person in 1942 – sugar, tea, butter, margarine, lard, bacon and an egg. The list of rationed foods changed during the war.

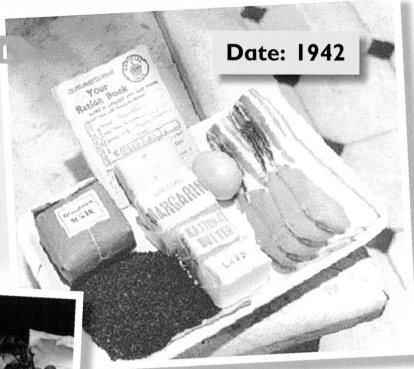

Date: 1942

A child uses her ration book to buy an orange. Oranges were in short supply so the government made sure that children bought them first, before adults.

Date: c. 1940

Be a history detective

- Look at the queue photo to find delivery bicycles. What sort of shop is Gunther's?
- Look for the clue that tells you who was allowed to buy oranges.

Growing food

Britain needed to grow more food itself, so the government told everyone to 'Dig for Victory'. Farmers ploughed up meadows to plant crops and produced as many animals as possible. Children helped to grow vegetables and fruit in gardens and school yards.

Date: 1942

Boys dig up the ground on a bombsite to plant bean seeds. Bombsites, allotments, gardens and even parks became vegetable plots.

Date: 1940

A girl puts waste food into a pig food bin. Lorries came round to collect the waste food, treat it and feed it to pigs. Some people had their own pig to provide extra meat for the family.

PIG FOOD

WASTE FOOD
FOR THE FEEDING OF PIGS

Evacuees help a farmer to harvest the barley crop.

Date: 1940

Be a history detective

- How will the farmer transport the barley crop back to the farm?
- Look at how the children are dressed. How are their clothes different from yours?

Clothes rationing

Clothes rationing started in 1941, which meant people had to use clothing coupons to buy clothes. It was difficult for mothers to buy enough clothes for their growing children. They often had to mend clothes rather than buy new ones.

Date: 1943

A mother and child leave a clothing exchange. Here they have swapped some old clothes for wellington boots and a warm coat.

Date: 1943

Mothers learn how to mend clothes or make new clothes out of old ones at a 'Make Do and Mend' class. Children wore some strange clothes during the war, including coats made from blankets and dresses made from curtains.

Be a history detective

- Read all the notices by the clothing exchange doorway. Did people pay for the clothes?

- Look for the girl at the sewing class. What is her mother making or mending?

The war ends

In May 1945, Germany surrendered and the war in Europe ended. Huge celebrations started all over the country. In August, Japan surrendered and the world was at peace. About 55 million people around the world had died during the war.

Date: 1945

A Victory in Europe (VE) party in Ipswich. As the war came to an end, women saved up food rations to make a party for the children.

A soldier returns to his delighted family. It was difficult for some children to have their father home as they hardly knew him. For others, it was the happy ending they had always hoped for.

Date: 1945

Be a history detective

- Many soldiers returned to find that their homes had been destroyed by bombs. Look at the photo above to see what a prefab, a temporary home for bombed-out families, looked like.

- Why do you think there are hardly any men at the VE party?

World War II quiz

How much have you learnt? Try the quiz below to see. Look back through the book to check your answers.

1. When did the war start?
2. Who carried a gas mask?
3. What was the blackout?
4. Did children go to school?
5. Were clothes rationed?
6. What was evacuation?
7. What was the Blitz?
8. What did Land Girls do?
9. When did the war end?

The war changed many children's lives. Look back through the book to find some of the good times, and the bad. What would you have liked about living in wartime Britain, and what would you have hated?

Glossary

Air raid An attack by bomber planes.

Air-raid shelter A metal or brick shelter that provides protection during an air raid.

Air-raid warden Properly known as air-raid precaution (ARP) wardens, these men and women checked the blackout and helped during air raids.

Allotment A plot of land, next to many others, where people grow vegetables, fruit and flowers.

Armed forces The army, the navy or the airforce.

Blackout During the war, the government ordered a blackout so that no light could be seen by enemy pilots. People had to draw thick curtains at windows, cover car headlights and manage without street lights.

Blitz Air raids on British cities between September 1940 and May 1941.

Bombsite An area where buildings have been destroyed by bombs.

Evacuation Moving school children, children under the age of five and their mothers, and pregnant women to safer areas during the war.

Gas mask A rubber mask with a filter to stop the wearer from breathing in poison gas.

Land Army The women, called Land Girls, who helped farmers to grow food during the war.

Pitchfork A tool with a long handle and prongs at the end, used to move straw and hay.

Prefab A small house put together quickly from parts made in a factory. Prefabs were used to replace homes destroyed during air raids.

Ration book A book containing coupons which could be marked, cut out or torn out. It allowed the owner to buy rationed foods.

Siren A loud warning noise produced by a machine.

Submarine An underwater boat.

Surrender When one side gives up fighting in a war and says the other side has won.

Index

Further information

Books
Starting History: World War II
by Sally Hewitt (Franklin Watts)

Websites
www.iwm.org.uk/upload/package/20
/lifeinww2/index.htm
An Imperial War Museum website
about life in World War II.

www.iwm.org.uk/upload/package/19
/makemend/make_and_spend.htm
An interactive site from the Imperial
War Museum where you can learn
all about clothes rationing.

www.bbc.co.uk/history/ww2children/
index/shtml
This BBC schools website gives
information about children in World
War II, as well as on-line activities.

Note to parents and teachers: Every effort has been
made by the Publishers to ensure that these websites are
suitable for children, that they are of the highest
educational value, and that they contain no inappropriate
or offensive material. However, because of the nature of
the Internet, it is impossible to guarantee that the contents
of these sites will not be altered. We strongly advise that
Internet access is supervised by a responsible adult.